Pernod
the Creator of Absinthe

Marie-Claude Delahaye founded the MUSEE DE L'ABSINTHE in 1994 in Auvers-sur-Oise with her private collection.

Partial view of one of the upper-floor exhibition rooms

Other works by the same author are listed at the end of this book.
Books that are still in print can be purchased at the museum or by mail order.

MUSÉE DE L'ABSINTHE
44 rue Callé, 95430 AUVERS-SUR-OISE
T/F : +33 (0)1 30 36 83 26

Marie-Claude DELAHAYE

PERNOD

the Creator of Absinthe

Artemesia Collection
Special Edition

Musée de l'Absinthe
Auvers-sur-Oise
Édition

FONDÉE EN 1805 PARIS
FONDÉE EN 1805
PERNOD®
AUX EXTRAITS DE PLANTES D'
ABSINTHE
LONDON- PARIS
NEW YORK
SYDNEY-TOKYO
70 cl e
68% vol.
SPIRITUEUX AUX EXTRAITS DE PLANTES D'ABSINTHE

Contents

Bottle labels.
Past and present.

Water-colour postcard "*Un bon Pernod*!..."

I could happily compare absinthe to a hot-air balloon. It lifts one's spirits, as the balloon lifts the basket. It transports one's soul as the balloon transports its passengers. It broadens one's imagination as the balloon broadens the view of the earth's sphere. It is the flow that carries the dream, as the wind carries the balloon...

Raymond Queneau
Le Vol d'Icare, 1968.

Pernod Fils Absinthe

1805-1915

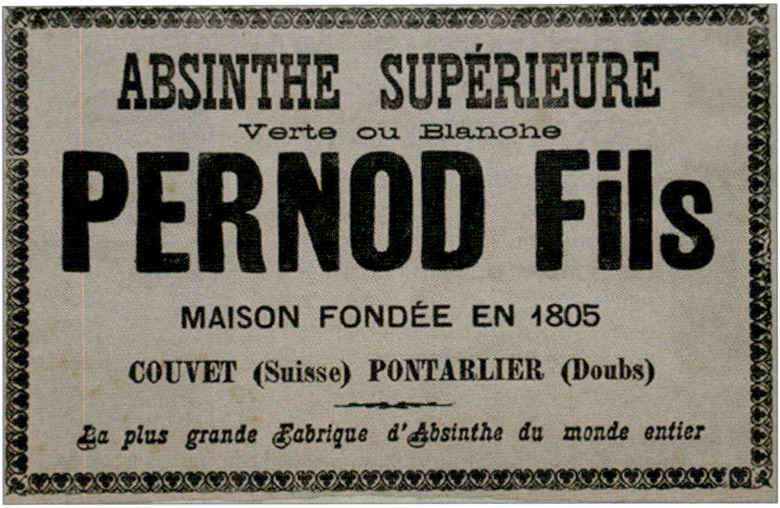

Blotter advertising Pernod Fils absinthe.

Antique miniatures of Pernod Fils absinthe.

Garçon! Bring me a Pernod!

This innocuous little phrase, tossed out into the warmth of a 19th Century café to order a *«Pernod Fils absinthe»*, shows just how well-known the brand was.

Pernod founded the very first absinthe distillery and promoted its name world-wide, exporting a French art de vivre along with its absinthe.

Two hundred years after its birth, Pernod absinthe has been re-designed by Pernod, taking the form of a new drink officially described as a *«Spirit with absinthe plant extracts»* which, while it meets current health regulations, has drawn its inspiration from the recipe of the past.

From past to present, an ancestral ritual: ice-cold water is dripped over sugar cubes placed on the absinthe spoon resting on the glass.

Pernod aux Plantes d'Absinthe Supérieure is a descendent of its distinguished ancestor, still retaining its original 68°. It is diluted with 6 to 7 measures of ice-cold and lightly sweetened water which gracefully clouds its pale green robe.

The poetry of the ritual

Absinthe is drunk diluted. The novelty of adding cold water to an alcoholic spirit gave birth to the ritual that makes absinthe an amusing social aperitif. A social ritual par excellence, lively conversation would spark up while the iridescent, opalescent spirals gently rose up the glass, expelling subtle aromas and filling the room with the powerful smell of aniseed.

The absinthe ritual is the prelude to a trio of pleasures combining the aesthetic, the olfactory and the pleasure of taste.

Water is dispensed from the small taps on the fountain drop by drop onto the sugar cubes.
The sweetened water then drips through the slots in the spoon into the absinthe, clouding it and causing it to turn an opal or emerald colour.

Always loosen it up
with a first drop...
There, there,
so softly.
Then you will see it
come to life,
ingenuously stimula-
ting smiles.
The water should be
as dew to it;
let it be known
waking its juices
gently,
slowly...
Raoul Ponchon 1891.

When your absinthe is poured
Into the bottom of a crystal glass
Place two broken rocks of sugar
One on top of the other,
On the metal spoon.

Then carefully pour
A fine stream of clear water.
Watch well; here's how.
So that it will not be bland
You must pour very slowly.

The absinthe will turn paler,
Will spread its divine aroma
And you will see in the whiteness
Of this subtle liquor,
Beautiful tints of amber and opal.

You will then have yourself
a perfectly formed absinthe;
Follow my lesson carefully;
If it goes to your head,
Sing a song
To calm your lively soul

These comic postcards date from around 1900 and it is no coincidence that they show a bottle of Pernod absinthe. A century after its creation, Pernod was by far the leading brand, with over a thousand other brands available on the market.

Objects used for the ritual

Spoons showing the absinthe leaf and the Eiffel Tower inaugurated in 1889.

Absinthe spoons

These are embellished with different openwork designs, from simple slots to more elaborate compositions.

They were made by silversmiths in pewter, nickel or ferrous metal for the smaller cafés, in nickel-silver and silver-plated metal for the grand cafés on the boulevards and in solid silver for bourgeois families.

Water pot

The small hole in the animal's mouth is used to pour a thin stream of ice-cold water onto the sugar. The water pot replaces the fountain.

The absinthe glass

Always taller and wider, since absinthe is diluted 6 to 7 times. It has a hollow bulge at its base to hold the dose of absinthe.

Topette bottle for Pernod absinthe.
Topette bottles were used to replace the commercial bottles on bourgeois tables.

Absinthe, a bouquet of flavours

The aromas that rise from a glass of Absinthe appeal to all the senses, arousing them while the different flavours caress the pallet. Aniseed - the most dominant - comes first, followed by the more subtle hyssop and melissa, leaving a final aftertaste of that secret, indefinable absinthe «je ne sais quoi».

So many plants and so many individual flavours which once combined, intermingle and collide on the pallet, before stretching out voluptuously, bringing the drinker nothing but pleasure.

Small colour print with advert on back.

Absinthe is undoubtedly at its most beautiful to the eyes and the tastebuds when its emerald liquid suddenly clouds into a milky opalescence and then releases vapours of melissa and aniseed, when it evokes images of freshness and spreads subtle perfumes at the hottest and heaviest part of the day, when it incites dreams of the splendid greens of striped sunsets of pale satin and the wild aromas of desert lands.

Jean Richepin

The liquor takes its name from one of its constituent plants, Artemisia absinthium, or Grand Wormwood.
The medicinal virtues of this perennial mountain plant from the artemesia family have been known since Antiquity. It has digestive, antipyretic, emmenagogic, antiseptic, tonic and stimulant properties and was taken in the form of an infusion or absinthe wine.
Grand Wormwood has greyish foliage, a highly aromatic smell and an extremely bitter taste.

Artemisia absinthium or grand wormwood owes its name to the Goddess Artemis, Goddess of the moon and Protector of women.

The characteristic aniseed flavour of absinthe comes from star anise, fennel and green anise to which melissa, hyssop or coriander may be added. Distillers would personalise their products by adding other plants or spices.

There are no names sweeter than those of the plants with which the clement liquor is distilled. And I know no other in the plant world that is more vivid and stands more proud. It is the flower itself of the nervous hyssop, the fennel in which the surmullets of kings is grilled, the melissa used to bring colour back to fainting women, the aniseed flavouring sensational dishes, the angelica bringing joy to children's gingerbread, the star anise grown by the Mandarin Chinese as the Dutch grow their tulips, the coriander that bleaches the saliva, the mint that chases out love, the oregano which brings shine to the eyes of virgins, then finally, the wormwood, grand or petite, the chaste finery of mountains and sea shores, daughter of the great pure winds, wheat of pure spaces and emblem of fierce freedom...

Ernest TISSERAND
À L'Ancre, Eloge de l'Absinthe, Paris, 1922

1805
Pernod Fils Absinthe

The legend traditionally attributes the creation of an absinthe elixir to Mother Henriod of Couvet of Val de Travers, in the Canton of Neuchâtel in Switzerland. She concocted it from plants that she found in the mountains. The elixir was then administered to the sick by a French doctor from Franche-Comté, Dr. Pierre Ordinaire.

A shrewd businessman named Major Dubied, saw that he could make considerable profit from this elixir. He bought the formula, but as a lace merchant he had no knowledge in the art of distilling, so he hired the young Henri-Louis Pernod to help him with the plant distillation. Henri-Louis Pernod was only 21 years old but was already working with his grower-distiller father. He assisted Major Dubied and his sons in setting up their distillery in Couvet, in 1798

Henri-Louis Pernod (1776-1851)
Portrait crowned with a sprig of absinthe, the source of his success.
Father and founder of the Pernod dynasty, Henri-Louis gave his name to a brand of international renown.

The business prospered and Henri-Louis Pernod decided to set up his own factory in Couvet in 1802. Despite successive extensions, the premises soon proved to be too small. To meet the growing demand of his French clientele who valued his elixir highly and to avoid the high customs duties that the French fiscal system levied on alcohol imported from Switzerland, Henri-Louis Pernod decided to set up on the other side of the border, in Pontarlier in the Doubs region.

With the small Couvet factory still running, Henri-Louis Pernod, aged only 29, found himself running two businesses.

The Couvet distillery was «a simple shack with two holes as windows and in all measuring eight metres long by four metres wide.».

On February 14th **1805**, Henri-Louis Pernod signed a lease for premises located in the *«main street in Pontarlier to set up a green water factory.».*

The Maison Pernod Fils was born.

Labels for Pernod Fils Absinthe, circa 1830.

With only two very well cared for shirts for luggage, Henri-Louis Pernod travelled around selling the products from his factory door-to-door.

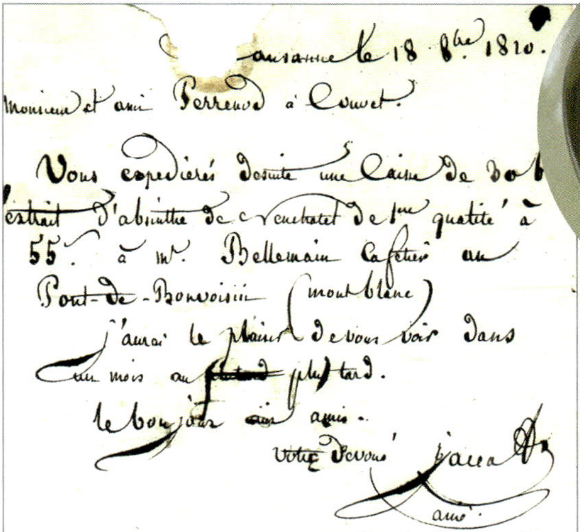
Lausanne le 18 8bre 1810.
Monsieur et ami Perrenod à Couvet.
Vous expédierés de suite une caisse de 30 b
extrait d'absinthe de concentraté de 1re qualité à
55 s. à Mr. Bellemain Cafetier au
Pont-de-Beauvoisin (mont blanc)
j'aurai le plaisir de vous voir dans
un mois au plus tard.
le bonjour à vos amis.
votre dévoué
ami.

Bottle blown for absinthe, 1830.

Letter-envelope dated 1810 addressed to M. Perrenod in Couvet with an order for 30 bottles of absinthe extract. (Pernod was originally written Perrenod).

Detail of the glass stamp at the base of the bottle neck. The ***Pernod Couvet and Pontarlier*** *brand figures both factory locations.*
The cross is a reminder of the founder's origins.

Henri-Louis was widowed in 1806. On May 25th 1807, he married Émélie Dubied, daughter of the Major with whom he had gone into partnership ten years earlier.

1830
Pernod Absinthe in the desert sands

Absinthe remained a regional drink for twenty-five years. Its consumption was limited to its zones of production, namely French-speaking Switzerland and Franche-Comté in France.

In 1830, the troops set out to conquest Algeria. They took Pernod absinthe, which was one of the rare brands on the market, with them. It was to accompany all the military campaigns because of the properties of the plants it contained: it could be used to purify polluted waters and to protect soldiers against malaria and dysentery.

Plate made by the Choisy-le-Roi pottery works

Crowned with glory and bringing the mysteries of the Orient back with them, the soldiers were much admired by the bourgeoisie. They would sit in the cafés on the Grands Boulevards, which had become a Mecca for absinthe.

Lithograph, circa 1860.

1840
Pernod Absinthe
Queen of the Parisian boulevards

This new favourite drink of the soldiers fascinated the bourgeoisie, who were soon able to discover absinthe for themselves. The café terraces from Antin to Montmartre throbbed with customers from five to seven o'clock in the evening, at what became known as the Heure Verte (Green Hour).

Drinking absinthe soon became a custom linking all social classes.
At the Heure Verte, festivity reigned and conversation flowed freely.
Absinthe and the ritual of its consumption established the pleasurable custom of relaxing with friends before dinner.

Engraved topette bottle **Absinthe Pernod**. Front and back view.

Drawing by Pierre Vidal, 1893.

The Heure Verte had become the time for an aperitif and remains to this day a much loved social custom.

Pernod,
A flourishing business

By 1840, absinthe had become THE fashionable drink. Chic and modern and nicknamed the Fée Verte (Green Fairy), by artists, it was a must in all the cafés.
Business doubled for the Pernods. Despite the emergence of new distilleries, particularly in the Pontarlier region, consumers were still asking for Pernod Fils absinthe, with its solid reputation and thirty years on the market behind it.
Louis, son of Henri-Louis assisted his father at the distillery. The company's growth was not affected by his premature death at the age of 38, nor by that of Henri-Louis four years later, in 1851.

Getting ready for deliveries

1855 : the succession

Émélie, the widow of founder Henri-Louis, ran the business until her grandsons Louis-Alfred and Fritz took over in 1855.

Louis-Alfred Pernod.

Fritz Pernod

Although Fritz Pernod had initially learnt the clock-making trade from different masters in Switzerland, he entered the family business, equipping it with ultra-modern industrial equipment with the help of an engineer named Borel.

The two brothers expanded the business considerably, making it France's leading distillery.

1877 : a model factory

By 1877, public demand for absinthe had reached new heights and the distillery's capacity was no longer adequate. The two brothers bought a piece of land beside the Doubs on which they constructed an exemplary factory a year later.

Overall view of the Pernod Fils factory. Dentu Monograph, 1896.

The factory was much admired by its visitors for its ultra-modern design and installations.
Two vast halls backed onto the $2,000m^2$ main building. One of the halls was used for incoming raw materials and the other, for merchandise ready for dispatch.

The generators room.

Pernod Fils Absinthe:
A high-quality absinthe

Pernod Fils absinthe was made by distilling aromatic plants after steeping them in spirits.

This process produced a higher quality absinthe than those obtained from a combination of plant essences with spirits of unknown origin.

Numerous drawings and photographs in postcard format show that the most modern processes were used throughout all stages of the production line, guaranteeing an exceptional quality.

The spirits in which the plants were steeped before being distilled arrived in wagons from the South of France. They were produced by distilling the surplus of Hérault, Gard and Aude wines. This spirit, known as «trois-six du Midi» had a better reputation than beet spirit and was used for higher quality absinthe.

The Grand wormwood used by the Maison Pernod Fils was grown in Val-de-Travers in Switzerland and around Pontarlier.

«La culture de l'absinthe». Postcards.
Absinthe farming required very careful attention. The ground had to be kept clean and aerated with frequent weeding.
Grand wormwood was picked between 15th June and 15th July in dry weather. It was harvested by cutting each plant at ground level using secateurs or pruning knives.

Dosing room at the Pernod Fils factory. Postcard.

After two to six weeks drying, the plants were stacked on drying racks. They were then cut into small fragments and packed into canvas bags.

The batching room was located above the distillery. Here, the plants and seeds were dosed and distributed directly into the stills via a system of track-mounted trolleys.

The sprayed plants were placed in stills and steeped in a mixture of 85° spirit and water for 24 to 48 hours. The water retained certain resinous substances, while the alcohol extracted the aromatic constituents.
Once the steeping process was complete, the stills were heated with steam for the actual distillation process.
The double rectification process used by Pernod was the key to high-quality absinthe. This process involved using the heart of the distillation for another cooking process, thereby eliminating any toxic volatile product.

The final absinthe produced contained the active constituents of plants and had 68° or 72° of alcohol by volume.

The absinthe was white when it came out of the still. Since consumers preferred green, the white was steeped in petite wormwood and hyssop to release their chlorophyll. Only high-quality absinthes were coloured, since the chlorophyll could only be stable in high-degree spirits.

The barrel room.
Here, 230 barrels contained recently distilled absinthe. With age, the acrid taste of fresh absinthe disappears, the aroma develops and the perfume becomes sweeter.

Bottling and dispatch room.
Bottles were filled at a rate of 20 per minute.
Once full, the bottles were corked and labelled. Their necks were dressed with a sheet of tin.

Shipment room.
A large quantity of absinthe was sold in bulk, in casks or in demi-johns. It was then delivered to merchants who bottled it themselves.

Female staff at the Maison Pernod Fils in Pontarlier, 1899-1900. Photograph by De Jongh Frères.

The Maison Pernod was well-known for looking after the well-being of its staff. All staff members, men and women alike, were entitled to a share of profits after one year of service in the establishment. The funds were placed in savings accounts and paid out with interest to workers on the day of their departure or transferred to their entitled beneficiaries in the event of death.

A brand with many symbols

The brand's characteristic symbols have been used for over two centuries and are instantly recognisable to the public.

Henri-Louis Pernod and his descendants never forgot their origins and their ties to Switzerland. The Swiss federal cross figures on all the labels.

The logo changes over time but the federal cross is always there. The hat with two feathers, a symbol of freedom, is that of William Tell; who refused to yield to the bailiff Gessler, representing the Austrian authority. Legend attributes the revolt that led to the unification of Switzerland to this episode.

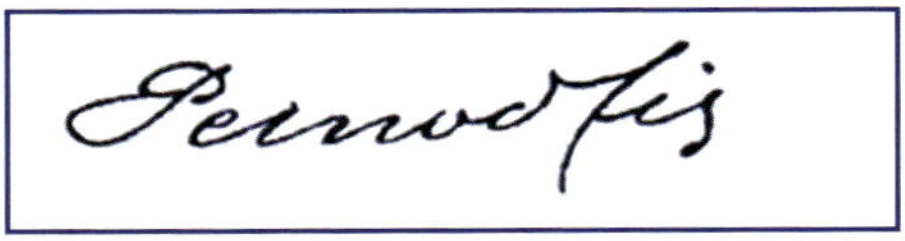

The Pernod Fils signature is a strong symbol of success. It still figures on the bottles today and is the essential link between generations, representing a continuity in quality over the years.

Trademark registration label.

The grape compositions on the label backgrounds are a reminder that Pernod Fils absinthe uses wine spirit only - a sign of quality.
A glass stamp bearing the brand name figures at the base of the bottle's neck.

The Pernod Saga

Edouard Pernod, the founder's eldest son, inherited the small Couvet distillery in Switzerland in 1827. In 1850, feeling too cramped, he set up a branch in Lunel in the Hérault.

Edouard retired in 1880, having signed the Couvet distillery over to Edouard Fils, who set up in Pontarlier in 1897.

The Lunel branch was taken over by his sister Louise who was married to Charles Gempp. It became the Maison Gempp Pernod.

Caroline, Edouard Pernod's second daughter, married Otto Legler, who seized the opportunity and set up a distillery in Couvet in 1864 and in Pontarlier in 1885. This was the Maison Legler Pernod.

With full rights to using the Pernod name, he exported worldwide, thereby strengthening the brand's impact.

Absinthe spoons engraved Edouard Pernod.

See pages 90,91, 92, art posters produced for these brands.

Details of the vase and its base. Relief engraving on the latter.

Fountain with six spouts. Engraved glass: «Absinthe supérieure Legler Pernod. Couvet & Pontarlier». Engraving on the base: «Legler Pernod à Couvet (Suisse) et Pontarlier (France)».

Pernod beyond the seas

In 1827, Henri-Louis wanted to extend his empire and assigned the management of the Couvet distillery to his eldest son from his first marriage, Edouard, while Louis, born from his union with Émélie Dubied, assisted him in the Pontarlier distillery. The markets were distributed evenly : Edouard exported to the States while Henri-Louis sold in France and the colonies.

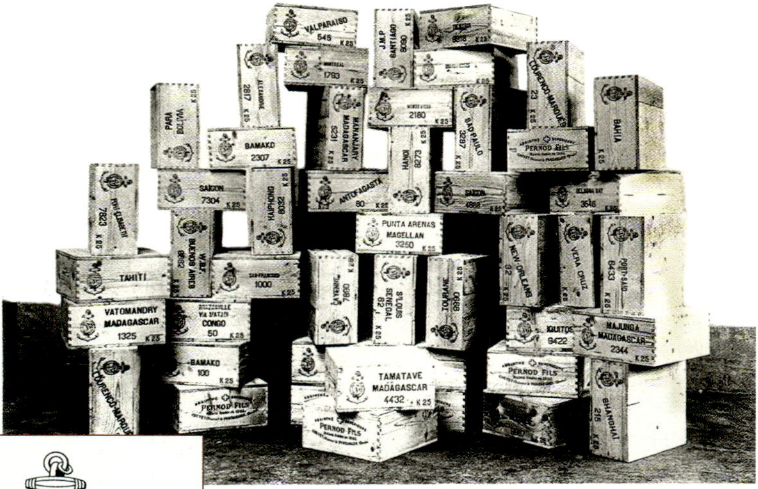

Cases marked with the name of countries all around the world, ready for dispatch: USA, Brazil, Senegal, China, Madagascar...

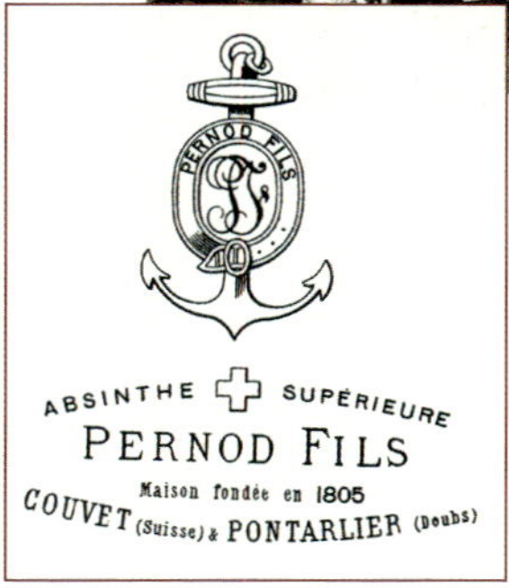

The ship's anchor with a PF in the centre is a clear indication that Pernod Fils absinthe was exported overseas.

Chest made from a case panel branded for export.

Advertising poster for exports.

Pernod Fils Green bottle and advertising brochure destined for England.

Bottle labels destined for export to South America and the USA.

Absinthe was enjoyed in the United-States, particularly in New Orleans where it was served at the Old Absinthe House. It was the main ingredient in cocktails such as the Sazérac, a mixture of absinthe and cognac, which was later replaced with bourbon. There was a real local absinthe culture, one that continued with the creation of the absinthe substitute Herbsaint in 1934.

Postcard of the Old Absinthe House in New Orleans, 1910.

All far-off voyages at the time were made on three-masted barques that usually left from Bordeaux or Nantes. Their holds would bulge with all the goods destined for the soldiers and colonists and they would come back laden with products from the countries they visited, particularly sugar and spices. We know the most common destinations from the bills of lading: Guadeloupe, Saint-Pierre de la Martinique, Cayenne.

A number of ships never actually reached their destination.

Such was the case for the Marie-Thérèse, the 1871 cargo which included 540 bottles of «E. Pernod Couvet» and «Pernod Fils» absinthe.

Detail of glass stamp on the bottle.

Pernod Fils bottle from the Marie-Thérèse shipment. This was found by submarine archaeologists in the «Gaspar Opération» team who brought up the wreck in May 1991.

The three-masted barque had left Bordeaux for Saigon but ran aground in the Gaspar Strait in the Indonesian sea. Surrounded by pirates, the ship was abandoned by the crew and sunk.

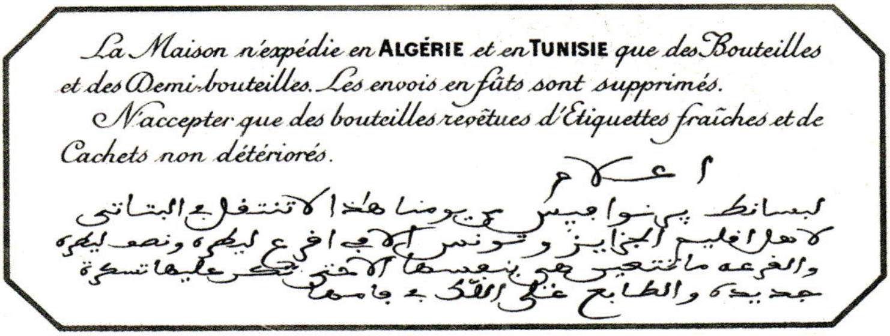
La Maison n'expédie en ALGÉRIE et en TUNISIE que des Bouteilles et des Demi-bouteilles. Les envois en fûts sont supprimés.
N'accepter que des bouteilles revêtues d'Etiquettes fraîches et de Cachets non détériorés.

Label for export to Algeria and Tunisia, destined to the troops and colonists.

I salute you, green-eyed fairy, dear Undine of the wretched devils,
Who has smiled upon us wherever the barrel is taken.
You and your friend tobacco, that little genie, black as powder, but such a dreamer and so good.
You bring us precious memories and even more precious lapses of memory.

Paul de Molènes, 1885.

Postcard. Senegal (Dakar)

1888
The Société Veil-Picard & Cie

Louis-Alfred Pernod ran the business alone after the death of his brother Fritz on May 17th 1880 and continued to invest in the Pontarlier distillery, with the support of the Veil-Picard bank in Besançon. His responsibilities eventually became too much for him and he sold the factory to brothers Arthur-Georges and Edouard-Charles Veil-Picard on condition that they would continue to use the Pernod Fils trademark. He kept his position as factory director but was no longer responsible for administrative and financial matters. Whenever he could, he would retire to his château at Neuchâtel where he would devote himself to painting, his favourite activity.

La Marchandise voyage aux risques et périls du destinataire et pour les Expéditions outre mer l'assurance n'a lieu que sur son ordre exprès.

MAISON PERNOD FILS
VEIL-PICARD & C°
MAISON FONDÉE EN 1805
COUVET Suisse
PONTARLIER (Doubs)

le 13 Mai 1891

Monsieur P. Guyardeau, Negt,
passage Moirin Angers

D'après la demande que vous avez bien voulu nous faire par Mr Aubin
nous avons l'avantage de vous remettre facture aux marchandises détaillées ci-dessous et expédiées sous suite de frais par petite vitesse à Vr adresse en gare

Valeur 15 Juin pr en notre traite sans autre avis

Nous nous recommandons à la continuation de vos ordres, et vous présentons Monsieur, nos salutations empressées.

MAISON PERNOD FILS
p. pon. Veil-Picard & Cie

Veuillez adresser vos Lettres et vos Télégrammes :
MAISON PERNOD FILS
PONTARLIER

…s responsabilité pour les bonbonnes.

Pre-1901 invoices depict the factory with only one chimney.

Invoice dated 1891

1901
The factory in flames

On August 11th 1901, which happened to be the fire-brigade's feast day, the distillery was struck by lightening after a violent storm. The fluid raced through the iron structure of the goods-lift leading down to the cellars, burst open an absinthe-filled barrel, igniting the spirit which then spread the fire through the entire central cellar within a matter of seconds.

Madame Borel, the director's wife, was alone in the factory at the time and she ran for help immediately. Two employees had the hindsight to empty any still-intact vats of spirit and barrels of absinthe. Over a million litres were poured into the Doubs river.

The fire was roaring, the heat was unbearable and it is said that the parched firemen quenched their thirst with copious volumes of the cool absinthe that the water of the Doubs had become.

At four o'clock, the beams had collapsed and the fire continued to burn, spreading to another cellar.

Once the barrels and vats of alcohol had been destroyed, the alcohol formed a sheet of fire on the ground, burning with an intense heat.

Series of photo-cards relating the story of the factory fire.

On Monday evening, the cellar foyers were still burning and the roadside cellar windows continued to spit out long flames.
Four days later, on Thursday August 15th, smoke was still emanating from the factory site.

Besides turning molten bottles into works of art, the Pernod Fils factory fire also helped scientists to prove something that they had never before managed to prove, namely that the Loue was a tributary of the absinthe-transporting Doubs river.

Pernod Fils bottles melted by the fire.
The glass seal can be identified, as can the label encrusted in the mass of glass on the bottle on the left.

FIRE AT PERNOD FILS

Alas! What's this?
What do I hear?
What's this rumour
That has reached me?

What? The factory
Is in flames
Like resin itself
Oh my lord!

It's a mystery,
It's a plot
It's a crime
Against Pernod

...I'm being murdered,
They want me dead
I'm being cooked
A ghastly end

...Oh my absinthe
I so need it
That holy herb
Of fils Pernod,

...What can I drink
What shall I order?
How can I think
Of any subtler?

Than that absinthe
Next to which
Like colocynth
Are other drinks ...

Raoul Ponchon
Le Courrier Français,
1901.

-Dreadful, this Pontarlier fire business, throwing three hundred workers out into the streets!
André - Let's just hope it doesn't make the price of absinthe go up!...

Drawing by J. Belon.
L'Album de l'Intransigeant, 1901.
The illustrator gibes at General André, politician and minister of war, well-known for his penchant for absinthe.

1903
A new factory

Even though the factory had burnt down, business continued. Advertisements were published in various different newspapers informing consumers that they could still order their favourite brand.

LA MAISON PERNOD FILS

La Maison Pernod fils, de Pontarlier, informe sa nombreuse clientèle que, malgré l'incendie qui a détruit une partie de son usine, les immenses réserves contenues dans les magasins épargnés par le feu et les approvisionnements considérables qui se trouvent dans ses dépôts lui permettent d'exécuter toutes les commandes, quelle que soit leur importance.

Grâce aux mesures prises immédiatement par la Maison, la fabrication, interrompue, pendant quelques jours, a recommencé. La clientèle est assurée de recevoir le même produit avec la même promptitude et la même régularité que par le passé.

Advert in *Le Journal*, 1903.

The factory ruins were soon cleared and reconstruction works began. The new distillery was to be the pride of the brand. It was larger and had an overall better design, equipped with ultra-modern equipment.
The different factory installations are shown in a number of postcards.

Partial view of the factory, on the Doubs.
The residential section can be seen on the left.

One of the distillery aisles.

Bottle rinsing facility.

Dispatch line. Packaging.

Price book for sales representatives. Front and back.

The cover shows both the brand's representative signature while the anchor containing the letters PF is printed on the front.
The back features the brand's well-known symbols: the label with the federal cross topped with the feather hat and a reproduction of the wax seal on the cork.

MAISON PERNOD FILS
FONDÉE EN 1805
VEIL-PICARD & Cie
PONTARLIER (Doubs) & COUVET (Suisse)

Pontarlier, le 14 novembre 1911.

Sté du Café de l'Univers
Limoges.

Doit

Adresser Lettres et Télégrammes MAISON PERNOD FILS PONTARLIER

pour les marchandises détaillées ci-dessous et livrées par notre Dépôt
suivant ordre de n/ Représentant M.
Valeur 15 Décembre contre notre traite sans autre avis

Les marchandises sont payables dans PONTARLIER

50 bout. vrac

Invoice dated 1911. The letterhead shows the new factory with its two chimneys. The ship anchor is now printed on all documents.

Partial view of a still-full antique bottle. Pernod Fils absinthe was only sold in seal-stamped bottles to prevent fraud. It was available at 68 or 72°, green or white.

On these postcards, the Pernod Fils absinthe inscription is given prime position in the window. Quality absinthe made only with wine-based spirits, higher priced than other more commonplace absinthes.

From the Green Fairy to the Green Peril

Initially, absinthe was a fashionable drink, essentially drunk by soldiers, the bourgeoisie and artists. It ended up falling victim to its extreme popularity. It hit the streets around the 1860s, attracting workers who would get drunk on cheap imitations made with poor quality alcohol. A number of imitation brands were available on the market and adulterated absinthe caused just as much harm as excessive drinking.

The Green drink
Beware of that green drink
Which, scruple-free and knowingly
is lavished on the innocent crowds
In your thousands of taverns!...
Auguste Jolly, 1898

Increased Consumption

Because of the growing popularity of absinthe, an increasing number of distilleries were opening to cater for a growing demand in alcohol. Bars opened on every street corner: there were no fewer than 480,000 in 1909, one for every thirty adult males.

The surge in alcoholism, which was a result of social misery, attracted the attention of health-workers and economists. They blamed the malady for most illnesses of the digestive and nervous systems, and absinthe bore the brunt of the blame. It soon became the symbol of alcoholism and would remain so for many years.

-Well, you want me to tell you ... You're a good guy, so you go buy us a Pernod.

Drawing by Ricardo Florès, featured in *La Caricature*, 1900.

Absinthism

This was the French Académie de Médécine's term for the physiological phenomena caused by absinthe consumption, which for them indicated a serious state of alcoholism.
The numerous manifestations of excessive irritability, tactile hypersensitivity, muscular tension and, at a more advanced stage, convulsions and epileptic fits, were thought to be caused by a molecule that made up 60% of grand wormwood's essential oil, thuyone.

The toxicity of absinthe essence, especially of thuyone, was tested on animals with results that are considered widely disputable today.

The fight against alcoholism

A serious movement towards banning absinthe began in 1880, under the aegis of newly-formed anti-alcoholic leagues. They fought for and obtained the support of famous literary, scientific and political institutions. A general outcry against the Green Fairy emerged : *Down with absinthe !*

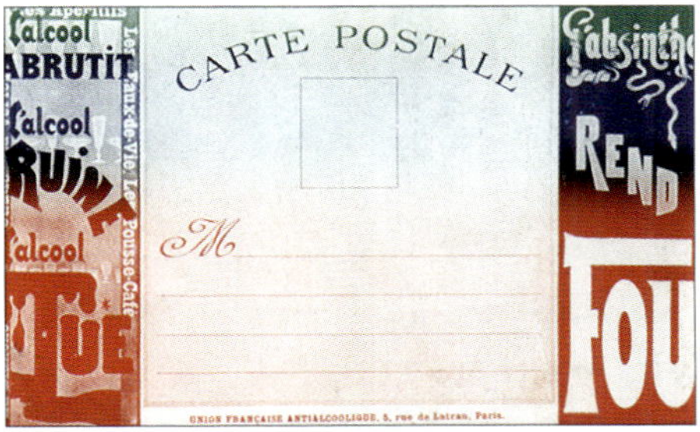

Postcard printed by the National French League against alcoholism

Wine industry in crisis

With over a thousand distilleries in a country where the wine industry was the livelihood of one person in six, absinthe was causing considerable economic tension.

La crise viticole (The wine crisis).
Drawing by Dufresne.
Illustrated supplement for the
Petit Journal, 1907.

The wine slump, which was caused by overproduction, triggered the crisis.

Thousands of wine growers, grouped together into very powerful unions, went up to Paris on June 8th, 1907 to demonstrate at the Trocadéro. The slogan launched by the newspaper Le Matin was clear: «***All for wine, all against absinthe !***»

1915
Prohibition

France had been at war since August 3rd 1914. Bordering countries such as Belgium and Switzerland had already banned absinthe in 1908 and 1910 respectively. In the face of public opinion, the State could no longer hold back. After forty years of discussion, twenty years introducing bills at the Chambers and the Senate and amendments to finance laws to aid the wine sector crisis, an initial decree was issued on January 7th 1915, valid for the duration of the war, followed by a definitive, unanimously approved decree on March 16th 1915.

- Reims? Anvers?
- No... Pernod!

Drawing by Léonce Burret.
Le Rire Rouge, 1914.

- Metz, Strasbourg, yes old mate, it's all very nice!...But who's gonna give us back Pernod?

Drawing by Noé.
Le Rire Rouge, 1918.

At the officer's table : Pernod Fils absinthe for aperitif.

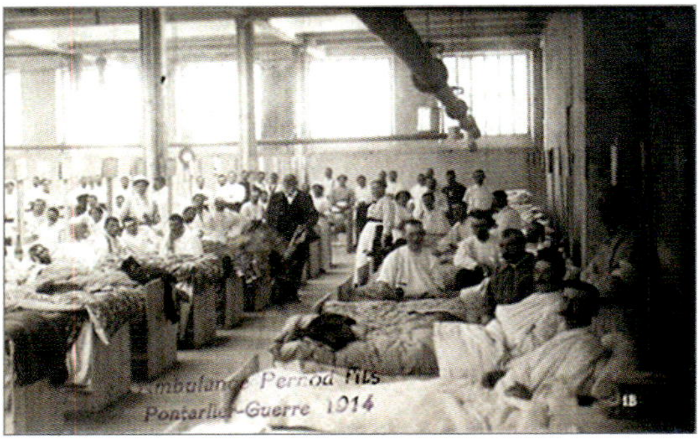

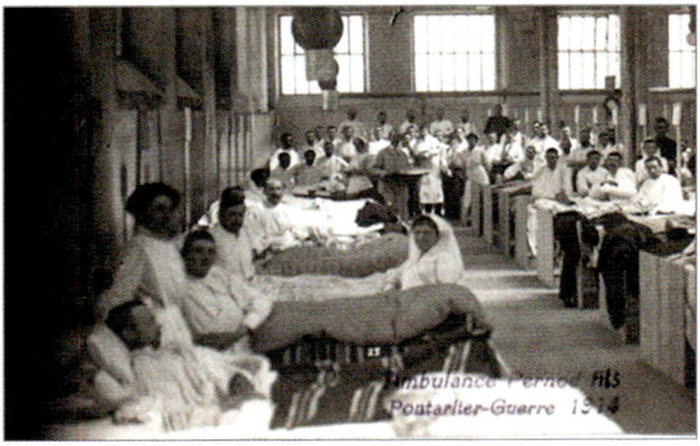

The Pernod Fils Pontarlier factory was transformed into a military hospital during WWI. Once the ban was in effect, it was sold to a chocolate manufacturer.

Postcards.

Poster by Gantner, 1915.

This poster depicts the Green Fairy being stabbed by the society of abstinence, the Blue Cross amidst wreathes brought by consumers. Raymond Poincaré, signatory of the decree, brandishes it triumphantly, war furies are depicted in the distance.

Postcard

1926
Revival of the Pernod Fils brand

After the 1915 ban, business had come to a complete halt in Pontarlier. It was pointless for the Veil-Picard brothers to keep a factory that was no longer producing, so they sold it. When anise-based liqueurs were sanctioned in 1922, they decided to revive their Pernod Fils brand. They offered it to André Hémard, owner of a flourishing business in Montreuil-sous-Bois in the Paris region. The merger took place on July 25th 1926.

The brand's characteristic symbols, such as the federal cross and the William Tell hat, were once again in use.

Ephemerid

Carafe decorated with the Charles Maire painting (see p.80), with mounted advertisements following the same principle as the original Charles Maire advertisement.

The absinthe spoon is tipped with the Pernod logo. It was made in 1927, on the occasion of the music-hall revue Adieu Tabarin.

1928
Etablissements Pernod

The Etablissements Pernod were born from the merger, on December 4th 1928, between Maison *A. Hémard et Pernod Fils Réunis* and Maison *Jules Pernod* in Avignon, a company that had been a major source of competition since 1876. In the 1930s, absinthe was replaced by anise-based spirits at 40°, however the ritual objects were still being used, evoking the brand's prestigious past for those who were nostalgic for the Green Fairy.

The Modern Era

Pernod at 45° was born in 1938.

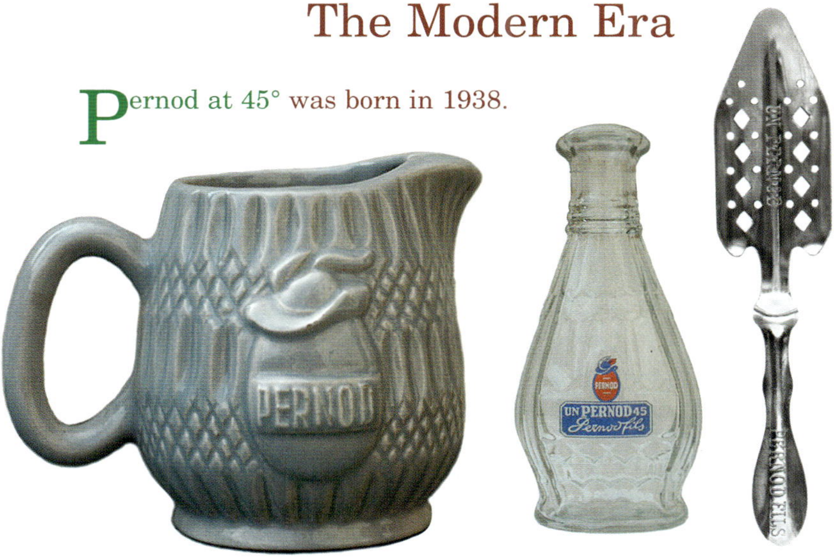

In 1938, absinthe spoons were still being used in cafés to serve Pernod in the traditional manner.

It continued proudly through the decades, awaiting the return of absinthe, despite competition in 1951 from Pastis 51, the Pernod Company's "Pastis", which had become the new national drink.
Pernod nevertheless kept its charm, much-loved throughout the world.

Poster designed for England, 1986.

2005 : The Bicentenary

Few companies can boast two centuries of operation under the same label.
The bicentenary Pernod bottle proudly displays its origins with the *Pernod Fils* signature.
Its contemporary design conveys a company well-anchored in the present and with a rich history behind it.

Pernod
Patron and Promoter
of the Arts

Absinthe
the muse of all arts

Poets, writers and artists, forever curious and always seeking out new sources of pleasure, succumbed to the charms of the Green Fairy and made it their muse. They lived in the cafés, which were warmer than their garrets, where, further heated by abundant libations, they would discuss, work and recite poetry.
Despite the immense diversity of cafés, each group of artists had its own preferences and haunts. In 1830, bohemian writers and poets took over the Latin Quarter in Paris. Musset, who was well-placed at the Procope café, set the tone. An inveterate chess player, he punctuated his games with beer and absinthe. After 1860, the bohemians moved on towards the more animated cafés of the Grands Boulevards, from the Bastille to Montmartre.

Paul Verlaine, by Cesare Bacchi.

For me, my glory is but a humble ephemeral absinthe
drunk on the sly, with fear of treason
and if I drink no longer, it is for good reason

Paul Verlaine.

Many artists, from Daumier to Picasso, produced series of cafe scenes reflecting contemporary concerns. The ambiance would vary depending on the artist, taking the viewer from the bohemian cafés frequented by the likes of Degas, Devambez and Evenepoel, through the boulevard cafés of Béraud and Toulouse-Lautrec, to the dingy haunts of Daumier or Raffaëlli.

Edouard Manet, (1832-1883).
Le buveur d'absinthe, 1859.
Etching and aquatint.
Carlsberg Glypothek Museum in Copenhagen.

Manet's Le buveur d'absinthe, was eliminated unanimously, minus Delacroix's voice, at the 1859 Salon. Manet used the simple rag-man Collardet, who used to beg on the steps of the Louvre palace, as his model. This first version was touched up by Manet in 1867, then in 1872.

> The first stage is like ordinary drinking, the second when you begin to see monstrous and cruel things, but if you can persevere you will enter in upon the third stage where you see things that you want to see, wonderful curious things.
>
> Oscar Wilde

Edgar Degas (1834-1917)
Dans un café ou l'Absinthe, 1876.
Oil on canvas.
Musée d'Orsay, Paris.

This painting is set in La Nouvelle Athènes café. Ellen André, theatre actress and Marcellin Desboutin, painter and engraver, both well known in bohemian circles and friends of Degas, were accused of being «fools» by the harsh critics. During an interview given in her lodge at the Edouard VII theatre, Ellen André stated that: «Our only role was to look into the vague distance like two idiots!». A role, she admitted, that would not be any good for her career.

Jean Béraud (1849-1935)
Le buveur d'absinthe, 1908.
Oil on wood. Private collection.

Béraud painted Parisian-type scenes and was particularly fond of café interiors where absinthe was always present. Associated with billiards or backgammon, it emerged as the favourite drink of the low life.
The scene is reminiscent of the Degas painting : the man and the woman are seated together without seeing each other, lost in their own solitude.

Henri de Toulouse-Lautrec (1864-1901)
Monsieur Boileau au café, 1893.
Peinture à l'essence on board. Cleveland Museum of Art, Hinman B. Hurlbut Collection.

Toulouse-Lautrec was an adept of «earthquakes», a cocktail of absinthe and cognac, and never went anywhere without his custom-made cane which contained a small phial and a glass. A great amateur of whores and brothels, he nevertheless portrayed absinthe as a drink for the Bourgeoisie.

Vincent van Gogh (1853-1890)
L'Absinthe, 1887. Oil on canvas. Van Gogh Museum, Amsterdam.

Absinthe, a major presence in van Gogh's life, was no less a one in his paintings: that presence could be obvious, as in this painting, or more subtle, as in *Café de nuit à Arles* (1888). He drank absinthe diluted with water in the cafés, and he found the cloudy substance so attractive that he wrote a letter to his brother: «*...I have a view of the Rhône, in which the sky and the river are the colour of absinthe, with a blue bridge and blackish figures...*»

Pernod Fils Absinthe, Source of inspiration

The notoriety of Pernod Fils absinthe was such that it naturally inspired many still lifes.

L'Heure verte.
Oil on canvas by **V. Cros**, 1895.
Musée de l'Absinthe. Auvers-sur-Oise.

L'Heure Verte.
Oil on canvas by **Belin**, 1896.
Musée municipal de Pontarlier.

Anxious and despondent, in the smoke-filled
Café I dreamt, and, dreaming, I put into verse
The blue tones of the sun that I loved as a poet
When I saw his very beams in a glass of absinthe …

Edmond Bourgeois.

L'Absinthe.
Oil on canvas by **Girardot Aîné**, 1883.

A glass of Absinthe is as poetic as anything in the world.
What difference is there between a glass of Absinthe and a sunset ?

Oscar Wilde

L'Absinthe.
Oil on canvas signed **Triolet**.

The most famous still life depicting Absinthe is the one painted by **Charles Maire**, a painter from Pontarlier who died in the common ward of the hospital in 1919, and who remained unknown, apart from the canvas that he was commissioned to paint by the Maison Pernod. Destined to adorn café walls across France, it was reproduced in the form of lithographs on canvas in thousands of copies.

These were framed at the factory in a workshop that had been set up specifically for the purpose.

Mitre saw for framing mounted advertisements.

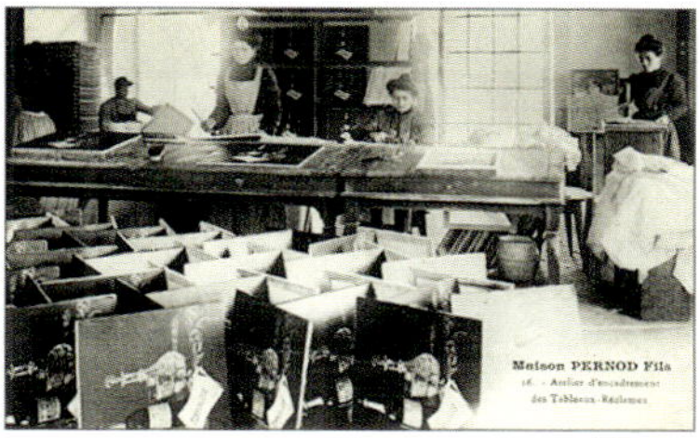

Framing workshop. Postcard.

This work gained additional fame when Picasso bought a print and gave it to his friend, the poet Jean Cocteau who hung it in his dining room in Milly-la-Forêt.

In 1959 in Paris-Match he was quoted as saying that this work: «*went down in the history of contemporary art the day that Picasso and Braque used it as inspiration for cubist still-life works*».

Colour lithography of the **Charles Maire** painting. Circa 1900. Musée de l'Absinthe. Auvers-sur-Oise.

Picasso's painting depicts the bottle, the floral tablecloth and the newspaper present in the Charles Maire painting. Picasso added an extra touch: a sugar placed on an absinthe spoon resting on the glass.

Jean Cocteau added «*The print that can be seen in my small dining room at Milly-la-Forêt is the original one offered to me by Picasso as a gift*». By «original», Cocteau means «the very one» that Picasso had given him, because the original canvas by Charles Maire has never been found.

Pablo Picasso. (1881-1973)
Bouteille de Pernod et verre, 1912. Oil on canvas (46 x 33 cm).
Musée de l'Ermitage, Saint-Petersburg.

Pablo Picasso. *Paysage aux affiches*, 1912.
Oil on canvas (46 x 61 cm).
The National Museum of Art, Tokyo.

l'Absinthe.
Oil on canvas, signed **Girard**. Circa 1900.

Artists were sensitive to the concerns of their time and didn't fail to denounce issues of alcoholism in their works towards the end of the 19th Century. The flip-side of fame - the bottle of Pernod absinthe had become a symbol for this alcoholism.

Jean d'Esparbès (1899-1968). *). Self portrait with absinthe. Musée de l'Absinthe. Auvers-sur-Oise.*

Liquid emerald of the waters shaded with amber
That in the pensive North is drunk around the fire,
Absinthe, poison green, hashish that makes even God,
Jealous of man, like a wild bucking steed...
Eugène Vermesch

Khristian Zhartmann (1843-1917).
L'Absinthe sur la terrasse, 1908.
Musée de l'Absinthe. Auvers-sur-Oise.

Although harmless at a first glance, this painting is rife with symbolism. Under the terrace awning, l'Heure Verte has rung and Pernod Fils absinthe awaits us.

Opposite the viewer, a woman is carrying a tray with a glass of absinthe in the shadows of the hotel doorway. Her face evokes death. Through this allegory, the artist seems to be calling upon our observational skills to appeal to our conscience, for although absinthe is a pleasant moment of relaxation, once the threshold of rationality - symbolised by the barrier - has been crossed, we will be heading straight for death.

Frédéric Deschamps (1849-1912).
En attendant l'Heure Verte. Pastel.
Musée de l'Absinthe. Auvers-sur-Oise.

Absinthe became a timeless legend and has continued to inspire artists until the present day.

Detail showing Pernod Fils engraved on one of the spoon handles (top right).

César (César Baldiccini dit) (1921-1998)
L'Absinthe, portrait de compression, 1998.
Musée de l'Absinthe. Auvers-sur-Oise.
Copyright Adagp, 2008.
Hundreds of antique spoons were used to create this original work.

Art at the service of Advertising : the Posters

At the beginning of the 19th Century, advertising came mainly in the form of leaflets or press inserts. It wasn't until the second half of the 19th Century, when cultural life became more intense and many new products arrived on the market, simultaneous to the development of lithography, that advertising started to be produced in poster format.

Art posters appeared in the advertising world in the 1870s, with the first colour lithographs by graphic designer and lithographer Jules Chéret. Street posters were originally for artistic purposes only, but advertising gradually became more common in the 1890s. This form of advertising was so greatly appreciated by the public that the best illustrators of the time were commissioned by manufacturers to promote their brands.

Morris Column covered with advertising posters, Boulevard Montmartre.
La Vie Parisienne, 1899.
Note the presence of the Edouard Pernod poster, centre right.

Lithograph poster, signed bottom left **Tamagno et Gallice**, 1906.
157 x 55 cm.
Printed by *P. Vercasson & Cie*, 43 rue de Lancry. Paris.
Musée de l'Absinthe.
Auvers-sur-Oise.

Tamagno (1862 - ?) studied at the Beaux-Arts in his birth town Turin, then in Rome before moving to Paris. He worked at the Camis printing house from 1890 to 1900, creating over a hundred posters.
As requested by Camis, Tamagno used actors and actresses as his models. He portrayed Sarah Bernhart and Coquelin Aîné for the *Absinthe Terminus* poster and François-Joseph Dailly for *Absinthe Cusenier*.
Tamagno left the Camis printing house to join **A. Gallice** in 1905, with whom he signed the Absinthe *Edouard Pernod poster*.
He left the lithographer Gallice in 1908 to work with the printer Pécaud.
His last known poster dates from 1927.

Lithographed poster signed bottom left **V. Leydet**, 1912.
Printed by *La Lithographie Nouvelle.* Asnières. 117 x 143 cm.
Pontarlier Musée municipal d'art et histoire.

V. Leydet shares the satisfaction of a well-filled day with the public. The great smile under the model's thick moustache, sleeves rolled up, lowered braces, a straw hat and the way he sits astride his chair, convey the relaxation of aperitif time, after may hard hours labouring the fields or the Languedoc vineyards

Leonetto Cappiello (1875-1942)) was one of the more gifted poster designers of his time. He didn't go in for the convoluted, overloaded and illegible style of posters of the time. He advocated simplicity and clarity. His creations reached their target so well that he is now considered to be one of the precursors of the graphics used in modern advertising. Cappiello also created the décor for the tea rooms at Galeries Lafayettes in 1912.

See Gempp Pernod and Édouard Pernod, page 38.

Lithographed poster signed **Leonetto Cappiello**, 1901, top right.
194 x 135 cm. Printed by *P. Vercasson & Cie,* 43 rue de Lancry, Paris.
Musée de l'Absinthe. Auvers-sur-Oise. Copyright Adagp, 2008.

French Ballad to the Glory of Pernod

My French Bacchus, God who reigns over the most glorious of wines, Bordeaux and Bourgogne, even Anjou, and Champagne, home to the pleasure of the heavens, with the purest tones of my lyre (which I translate into words) I implore you : to your empire add the celestial PERNOD.
A horrible green, eh ! It is not, but opalescent and velvety smooth, the Nectar that down here we name with the unison of six enchanted letters: PERNOD ! This liquor has no ruse, made with the purest of herbs, and which, if drunk in quantity, turns the universe to poetry !
Yes, the universe. With fancy-free and roaming mood - as much as these exquisite wines, has the whole world not surrendered to it ?
So long live Pernod ! Your charm, glorious aperitif, bears the flag leading the arms of the Spirit to victory.
All - squires, sailors, workers, kings, queens, State presidents, vagrants, bowing diplomats, Icelandic fishermen etcetera...
are your human adorers, Fils-Pernod, so many of them, oh yes!
Joining hands after drinking, they would tour the world,
then dancing, singing your praises, would tour Paradise, with the angels and God himself in their train, I tell you [...]
but that said, and a rumbling noise soon rises : pure Pernod, radiant Pernod, Pernod from Montmartre to Golconde and from Samarcande to Lisieux,
Pernod in a thousand and one places, Pernod right to the New World, Pernod right to the end of the worlds, Pernod right to the very heavens !

Paul Fort Prince of Poets

Poster signed and dated bottom right **A.M. Cassandre**, 1934.
Alliance graphique L. Danel. 34, rue Marc Seguin, Paris.
201 x 105 cm. Pernod Ricard collection.

In this photo-montage, the joyful face of the consumer fills both the bottle and the glass, showing the intimate bond between him and the product. Cassandre, a resolutely modern poster artist, finished the upper outline of the face with the curve of the bottle and letters forming the word Pernod.

Poster by **frères Gorsky** photographers. 1930.
Printed by *Henon*. Paris. 42 x 29 cm.
Pernod-Ricard group collection.

In 1930, it was no longer absinthe but its successor, Pernod 40°.

In 1937, to boost the sales of absinthe, stocks that had been produced in 1913 but were in storage in Holland were sold in countries that were not subject to the prohibition, such as Spain, Portugal and England. The Etablissements Pernod entrusted their advertising campaign to poster artist André Wilquin. The stocks were transferred to the Le Havre warehouses where they were destroyed by wartime bombs.

Mounted lithographed poster by **André Wilquin**, 1937.
Signed bottom right. 36 x 27 cm.
Original frame.
Printed by *Max Courteau*, Paris.

Wilquin wanted to revive the noble reputation of absinthe, which had been subject to so much criticism, by portraying it as a chic drink for the elite set, such as the cavalry society, *Les Habits Rouges*, represented in this poster.

André Wilquin (1899-2000), started in 1916 as apprentice-retoucher for printer-publishers Draeger frères. He was promoted to the design department in 1918. In 1925, he decided on his undulating signature. He created a number of posters up until 1960, which were characterised by a freshness of hues that was present throughout all his work.

Pernod
Patron of the Arts

The brand's interest in arts really was an integral part of the company's culture. Already in 1884, Louis-Alfred Pernod, the founder's grandson, was described in the Panthéon de l'Industrie of October 5th, as «*a philanthropist doubled as an artist and an archaeologist: in Pontarlier he created an exquisite Algerian lounge from the curiosities which he brought back from his trips to Africa. He also founded a small Roman museum with the pieces discovered during the excavation works necessitated by the enlargement of his factory.*».

Postcard.

The Pernod directors were dedicated to keeping up their workers' good spirits and created a music club within the company named *l'Espérance*.
It played at all major company events and accompanied the yearly excursions in France and Switzerland that the company organised for all its employees.

L'Espérance fanfare, 1899-1900. Photo by De Jongh Frères.

From the 1930s onwards, when anise-based spirits at 40° were made legal again, the Pernod company launched into active patronage, a concept that cleverly combined support for artists with publicity for the brand.

Small handout distributed by Pernod.

The Etablissements Pernod's marching song, written by writer Georges Milton in 1933.
Words by Max-Blot. Music by Henri Goubier Fils.

Over the past twenty-five years, support for artists has involved music and above all contemporary art, with exhibitions, funding of catalogues and art contests. The latter consist in asking young artists to express themselves on the theme of the brand. In return, participating artists are acknowledged in a number of different ways.

In 1991, the «*Féri'Art*» contest was held for the occasion of the Nîmes Feria. Artworks from the contest were exhibited in the form of street banners, creating a giant open-air exhibition.

In 1993, Pernod launched the «*Pernod, liquid Art*» contest in New-York. The contest was reserved for young artists who had not yet been exhibited. It provided the top ten artists with the opportunity to exhibit their work in a New-York gallery.

Advertising campaign featured in Paper New-York art journal.
Pernod Archives.

In 2005, to celebrate the brand's bicentennial, a contemporary art contest was held with 14 artists selected by the exhibition commissioner, Patrick-Gilles Persin. All works were collated into a catalogue and the exhibition toured to a Paris gallery and to the 5 regional Pernod clubs.

1st prize : Tony SOULIÉ.
Tony Soulié is a well-known artist internationally and has held over 200 private exhibitions. His work is exhibited in leading international museums.

2nd prize tie :
Luis LEMOS
Copyright
Adagp, 2008.

2nd prize tie :
Esti LEVY
Copyright
Adagp, 2008.

Pernod and the revival of Absinthe

1997
Absinthe re-invented

The Czech Republic was the first country to put a strong green-coloured alcohol called «Absinthe» back on the market. Its import into England, which was not subject to a prohibition law, was a great concern for French distillers.

The 1988 decree

Because vermouth aperitifs contained Artemisia absinthium (wormwoood), as did several liquors of the Chartreuse or Bénédictine type, the French government was asked by the WHO (World Health Organisation) and the European Council to amend its prohibition law, prompting Michel Rocard to sign a decree authorising wormwood in spirits.

Thuyone restrictions

The presence of wormwood is subject to strict regulations in its component molecule, thuyone, which is considered to be a neurotoxin.

This must not exceed 10 mg/l or 35 mg/l depending on the type of spirit. The distiller is required to calculate the quantity of wormwood to be used to comply with these standards.

The degree of alcohol

While Pastis is at 45°, the new «absinthes», containing less anise, are assimilated to anise-based spirits and are not therefore subject to restrictions in terms of the degree of alcohol. They can be at 45°, 55°, 57°, 68° and 72°.

Official name in France

«*Absinthe*» cannot be used as a name in France, because the absinthe ban is still in force. This is why it is officially called «*Spirit with absinthe plants*» or «*Spirit with absinthe plant extracts*». This is totally inconsistent with countries such as Switzerland, for example, where the 1910 ban was lifted in March 2006 and «*absinthe*» can now be used as a name.

Nevertheless, there are no laws to prevent distillers from printing special labels for export, since the 1915 law authorized absinthe production for export.

The ritual

The ancestral ritual consisted in dripping ice-cold water onto sugar cubes (See p. 15). To revive this ritual, distillers are marketing reproductions of glasses, slotted spoons and fountains in parallel to their product, thereby reviving the fun tradition of the aperitif.

The ritual of the 3rd millennium.

This new manner of consuming absinthe is a heresy from the Eastern countries and is growing in popularity. It mainly concerns absinthes with a high degree of alcohol and doesn't allow for the gradual development of flavours during the dilution process.

Here, absinthe imbibes the sugar which is then set alight. A little water is poured until a cloudy liquid is obtained. This non-traditional ritual is considered a heresy by absinth «purists».

Pernod aux Plantes d'Absinthe Supérieure

In October 2001, Pernod delved back to its roots, launching a spirit on the international market based on the recipe that brought it its fame in the 19th century.

Pernod aux Plantes d'Absinthe Supérieure (in France, Pernod aux Extraits de Plantes d'Absinthe) is made from alcohol, extracts of grand and petite wormwood, star anise and several other plants, with no added sugar. Its alcohol degree is at 68° and its thuyone content is under 10 mg per litre, in compliance with French law. It is aimed at a public of connoisseurs seduced by the authentic, traditional serving ritual of pouring ice-cold water over the sugar lump on the slotted spoon.

The legendary Pernod brand has contributed to a revival of absinthe, which has been laying dormant for almost a hundred years and has returned to charm the palate and fuel the imagination.

New generation absinthe spoon.

Lithographed metal poster, 2004.

Drinking Pernod aux Plantes d'Absinthe Supérieure

Pernod aux Plantes d'Absinthe Supérieure is still consumed today in the traditional manner, with 1 measure of Pernod aux Plantes d'Absinthe Supérieure (3cl) diluted onto a sugar cube.

It is also increasingly served in cocktails.
In addition to the traditional Perroquet, Tomate and Mauresque, which consist of adding a dash of mint, grenadine or orgeat syrup to absinthe or, more recently, Pastis, a number of today's cocktails are based on historical preparations.

The Sazerac

Born in New-Orleans in the first half of the 19th Century, this seems to be the oldest cocktail.
In an "old-fashioned" glass, mix 2 measures of rye Whisky, 1 dash of Pernod aux Plantes d'Absinthe Supérieure, a 1/2 spoonful of sugar and a dash of bitters (Peychaud or Angostura).

Earthquake

Invented by Toulouse-Lautrec for singer Yvette Guilbert and

singer-songwriter Aristide Bruant.
In an "old-fashioned" glass, mix 2 measures of Pernod aux Plantes d'Absinthe Supérieure and 1 dash of cognac. Add 5 volumes of ice-cold water dripped onto a sugar cube.

Many «mixologists» have drawn inspiration from these historical mixes, re-inventing new cocktails.

The Baudelaire

In a shaker, mix 1 measure of Pernod aux Plantes d'Absinthe Supérieure, 1/2 measure of Triple sec, the juice of 1 lemon and crushed ice. Shake well and serve as a «frappé» in a cocktail glass.

The Green Fairy

Mix 1/2 glass of crushed ice, 1 measure of Pernod aux Plantes d'Absinthe Supérieure, 1/2 measure of mint liqueur, 1 measure of vodka. Garnish with mint leaves.

Recreating the traditional Absinthe ritual.

Photo credits
(r: right; l: left; t: top; b: bottom; m: middle)◊◊
Jean-François **Bitaud**, p. 10, 45b, 48t, 55t, 66.
Jacky **Dacheux**, p. 12t, 28, 35t, 68br, 97t.
Marie-Claude **Delahaye-Musée de l'Absinthe**, p. 6,9,14, 15, 16, 18, 19, 21, 22, 23, 24, 25, 27, 30, 31, 32, 33, 34, 35b, 36, 37, 38, 40, 42t, 43, 44, 45t, 46, 47, 48m, 51, 52, 53, 54h, 57, 59, 60, 61, 62, 63,67rt, 68lb, 69t, 72, 79, 80, 84, 85 86, 87, 88, 89, 91, 95l, 96, 97b, 103.
Claude **Durand**, p. 12b, 26.
Green Utopia Ltd, p. 103.
Lili **Jacquet-Pierroulet**, 64m and b, 65.
Jean-André **Maragi** et Sylviane **Lisle**, p. 48b, 49, 58, 67l.
David **Nathan-Maister**, p. 39, 42bl, 55b, 56t.
Société **Pernod**, p. 13, 69b, 70, 93, 94, 98, 99, 100, 104, 105, 106, 107.
Yannick **Prodhomme**, p. 29.
Peter **Schaff**, 56b.
Olivier **Talfumière**, p. 41.
Charly **Walburger**, p. 17, 69tr, 96r.
Pascal **Wang**. p. 42br.
Collections privées, p. 64t, 77, 78, 83, 106.
References for artworks are provided beneath each piece individually.

Layout : Marie-Claude Delahaye
Total number of photos : 160

Translation : Polly Mc Donnell
Published by : Musée de l'Absinthe
44 rue Callé F-95430 Auvers-sur-Oise
T./F. 01.30.36.83.26.
Chief editor : Marie-Claude Delahaye.

Acknowledgements

I would like to thank Société Pernod for their faith in me and for allowing me to tell their story with full autonomy. I would particularly like to thank **Pierre Coppéré**, CEO of Société Pernod who has supported the project with enthusiasm; **Jean-François Collobert** and **Claudine Eynaud**, Managers of Pernod International and project initiators, with whom I worked in close collaboration. Product Manager **Charles de Saint Vincent** whose suggestions have been most valuable to me.
I would also like to thank all the museums and collectors, quoted in the photo credits, who were happy to share their collections with the public to further knowledge on the subject of absinthe and its creators, particularly Pernod.

Bibliography

Delahaye Marie-Claude, «*Pernod, un nom magique!*». *L'Absinthe, revue trimestrielle de recherches historiques*. Maisons-Alfort, published by Marie-Claude Delahaye, n°13, juin 1995.
Delahaye Marie-Claude, *L'Absinthe-muse des poètes*, 2000; *L'absinthe-Son Histoire*, 2001; *L'Absinthe-Les Cuillères*, 2001; *L'Absinthe-Les Affiches*, 2002. published by Musée de l'Absinthe, Auvers-sur-Oise.
Delahaye Marie-Claude *Pernod, 200 ans d'entreprise*, 2005. published by Musée de l'Absinthe, Auvers-sur-Oise.
Jequier François, «*La saga des Pernod : d'Henri-Louis à Louis-Alfred*». *Biographies neuchâteloises*. TIII. Hauterive, G. Attinger, 2001.

Du même auteur :
Collection Artemisia. Musée de l'Absinthe-édition
44 rue Callé 95430 Auvers-sur-Oise. T/F : 01.30.36.83.26

1- ***L'Absinthe muse des poètes***. 2000
302 p., 140 ph.

2- ***L'Absinthe Les cuillères***. 2001
319 p., 700 ph.

3- ***L'Absinthe Son Histoire***. 2001
335 p., 450 ph.

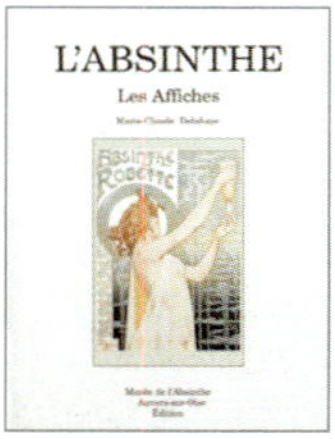

4- ***L'Absinthe Les Affiches.*** 2002
288 p., 330 ph.

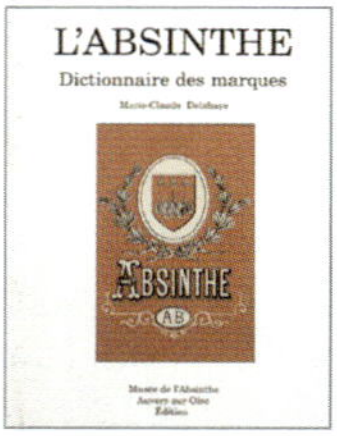

5- 1- ***L'Absinthe Dictionnaire des marques***. 2003.
Tome 1 : lettres **A** et **B**.
344 p., 665 ph.

6- ***L'Absinthe Ses dessinateurs de presse***. 2004
464 p., 473 ph.

5-Hs- ***Pernod, 200 ans d'entreprise***.
2005.
400 p., 995 ph.
Version anglaise.

5-2- ***L'Absinthe Dictionnaire des marques.*** 2006.
Tome 2 : lettre **C**.
360 p., 855 ph.

5-3- ***L'Absinthe Dictionnaire des marques.*** 2007
Tome 3 : lettres **D-E-F**.
352 p., 881 ph.

L'Absinthe, histoire de la Fée verte.
Paris, éd. Berger-Levrault, *1983*.
Deuxième édition en 1987.
Primé par l'Académie de médecine en 1986. Épuisé.

L'Absinthe, art et histoire.
Paris, éd. Trame Way, *1990*.
167 p., 440 photos.
Épuisé.

Le Livre du pastis.
Nice, Z'éditions, *1994*.
132 p., 250 photos.
Épuisé.

Absinthe, muse des peintres.
co-auteur : Benoît Noël.
Paris, éd. de l'Amateur, *1999*.
Épuisé.

L'Absinthe. Revue trimestrielle.
éd. Marie-Claude Delahaye.
Parution de 14 numéros, de *1992 à 1996*. Tirage à 300 exemplaires.
Au total 224 pages, 633 photos.

Petit traité de l'Absinthe Le mythe ressuscité.
St Rémy de Provence, éd. Équinoxe, *2003*.
Format 16,5 x 16,5.
176 p., 265 photos.
Version anglaise

Petit traité savant du pastis
St Rémy de Provence, éd. Équinoxe, *2005*
Format 16,5 x 16,5
176 p., 455 photos.

L'Absinthe au Féminin.
éd. Équinoxe, 2007.
136 p., 151ph.

Quatrième tirage

Achevé d'imprimer au mois de novembre 2010
sur les presses de
L'Imprimerie de la Centrale
62302 Lens
Dépôt légal : dernier trimestre 2010

ISBN 978-2-917507-01-8